EEVEE CROCHET KIT

EVERYTHING YOU NEED TO MAKE EEVEE AND INSTRUCTIONS FOR 5 OTHER POKÉMON

Sabrina Somers

T0386669

DAVID & CHARLES

www.davidandcharles.com

A DAVID AND CHARLES BOOK

©2024 Pokémon. ©1995–2024 Nintendo / Creatures Inc. / GAME FREAK inc. TM, ®, and character names are trademarks of Nintendo.

David and Charles is an imprint of David and Charles, Ltd. Suite A, Tourism House, Pynes Hill, Exeter, EX2 5WS

First published in the UK and USA in 2022

Sabrina Somers has asserted her right to be identified as author of this work in accordance with the Copyright, Designs and Patents Act, 1988.

Names of manufacturers and product ranges are provided for the information of readers, with no intention to infringe copyright or trademarks.

A catalogue record for this book is available from the British Library.

ISBN-13: 9781446309605

Printed, manufactured, and assembled, in Guangdong, China for David and Charles, Ltd
Suite A, Tourism House, Pynes Hill, Exeter, EX2 5WS

10 9 8 7 6 5

Publishing Director: Ame Verso
Head of Design: Anna Wade
Designer: Insight Design Concepts Ltd
Technical Editor: Carol Ibbetson
Photography: The Really Good Media Company
Packager: BlueRed Press Ltd

David and Charles publishes high-quality books on a wide range of subjects. For more information visit www.davidandcharles.com.

This book is part of the Eevee Crochet Kit and is not to be sold separately.

Figures on cover not to scale.

INTRODUCTION 4

TOOLS & MATERIALS 5

TECHNIQUES

TERMINOLOGY 7

HOW TO READ PATTERNS 7

BASIC CROCHET STITCHES

Magic Ring 8
Chain 9
Single Crochet 9
Slip Stitch 10
Increase 10
Decrease While Crocheting in Rounds 10
Decrease While Crocheting in Rows or Back Loops 11
Double Crochet 11
Half Double Crochet 12
Crochet in the Front or Back Loops 12

SPECIAL TECHNIQUES

Bind Off 12
Color Switch 13
Starting a Round with a Chain 13

MAKING UP

Closing a Piece 14
Crocheting Two Parts Together 14
Embroidery 15
Sewing Two Pieces Together 15

PROJECTS

BEGINNER
Pichu 16
Wobbuffet 20

EASY
Eevee 26
Pikachu 32
Meowth 36

INTERMEDIATE
Jolteon 40

MEET THE AUTHOR 48

INTRODUCTION

SKILL LEVELS

All Pokémon players need to train—themselves and their Pokémon. The same is true with crochet. To help in your training, the projects start with easy techniques. Later, they get a bit more difficult. For this kit I have designed six Pokémon for you to make. Which one will be your favorite?

A few words of advice—don't rush to do a difficult one until you have mastered the basics of crochet and construction. Start with an easy character, then go for it!

My Pokémon are presented in three levels of difficulty, each designated by a yellow line, the longer the line, the more difficult the crochet.

BEGINNER
The easiest are Pichu and Wobbuffet

EASY
The next group are Eevee, Pikachu, and Meowth.

INTERMEDIATE
Finally, the hardest Pokémon is Jolteon.

It doesn't matter whether you're a beginner or an expert, all of the patterns produce wonderful Pokémon! Keep them yourself—or give them as gifts.

I had great fun creating these patterns and I really hope that you enjoy making them too.

DIFFICULTY LEVELS
BEGINNER
EASY
INTERMEDIATE

WINDING A SKEIN INTO A BALL
STEP 1

To avoid your yarn tangling, it's highly recommended that you wind it into a ball before you begin. Winding yarn into a ball by hand is very simple. Unfold the skein so it forms one big loop. Begin by finding an end, wrap the yarn around three fingers a few dozen times. Carefully slide the yarn off your fingers keeping it neatly contained.

STEP 2

Fold the yarn in half over itself and continue to wind the string tightly around the tiny ball. It may look a little messy in the beginning, but as you continue to wind and turn the ball of yarn, it starts to take shape beautifully.

STEP 3

As you wind the yarn, be sure to twist the ball around to evenly distribute the yarn. Continue in this way until you have a ball!

TOOLS AND MATERIALS

CROCHET HOOK

There are numerous sizes of crochet hooks available, made of metal or plastic, and in several different lengths. You can simply change the size of your Pokémon by using a thicker or a smaller hook.

NOTE: It's very important to combine the thickness of the yarn with the correctly sized hook. On the label around the yarn you can find the recommended hook size. To create tight crochet work without big gaps—I recommend using a slightly smaller hook than indicated on the label.

TEXTILE MARKERS

Some Pokémon have eyes that are too small to cut from felt. In these cases you can put a dot in with a black textile marker instead.

YARN NEEDLE

After crocheting you'll need a needle to sew all the parts together. A large sewing needle is ideal. Alternatively, use a darning needle or tapestry needle—whichever you prefer.

FELT

To create the face and other small details on your Pokémon you need different color felts. Use thin felt for the best results; thick felt can look out of scale and clumsy.

PINS

Although pins are not really necessary, they can be very useful when making your Pokémon. By pinning all the parts together before sewing, you can decide how your Pokémon will stand, and change its posture if needed. But remember to take all the pins out afterward!

GLUE

You will need glue to stick the felt details to your Pokémon. Use a fabric glue for the most successful results. Make sure you cover the entire area with only a thin layer of glue—a thick layer will be visible through the felt.

FIBERFILL STUFFING

Fill your Pokémon with synthetic fiberfill, which is usually made of fluffed out polyester. Stuff your character firmly, but be particularly careful not to overfill it, as the yarn will stretch and the filling will be visible through the holes in the stitches. This spoils the effect.

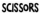

BRUSH

Used for fluffy parts—such as Eevee's collar—to fluff out the yarn. I recommend using a sharp brush with steel bristles. Failing that, a good hard bristle brush, or even an old toothbrush will do the trick.

SCISSORS

You will need scissors to cut off the yarn when you've finished and for cutting out the felt pieces. Some of the pieces are quite small and fiddly, so to get the best result with your felt, I heartily recommend small, sharp scissors.

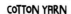

COTTON YARN

In the patterns I have specified the type of yarn I used. Personally, I like to work with cotton yarn, because it makes the crochet work look tight and neat, but you can use any kind of yarn or wool you feel comfortable with. For the fluffy parts, like the flames, it's better to use acrylic yarn as it unravels easily and can look really effective.

STITCH MARKERS

Most parts of the Pokémon are made in continuous rounds—you can't see a clear beginning or end. So, to keep track of the rounds, I recommend the use of a stitch marker. Place it at the end of the round: after crocheting the next round, you should end up right above the stitch marker. Now move the stitch marker up to the end of the last round. This way you will keep track of your pattern.

TECHNIQUES

TERMINOLOGY

In the book we are using US crochet terms.

ABBREVIATIONS

US	UK
CH – chain	**CH** – chain
TCH – turning chain	**TCH** – turning chain
SL.ST – slipstitch	**SL.ST** – slipstitch
SC – single crochet	**DC** – double crochet
HDC – half double crochet	**HTR** – half treble crochet
DC – double crochet	**TR** – treble crochet
TC – triple crochet	**DTR** – double triple crochet
DEC – decrease	**DEC** – decrease
RND – round	**RND** – round
ROW – row	**ROW** – row

NB. It is very important to distinguish between rounds and rows. Rounds go round and round and continue to work in the same direction, while rows are worked from side to side, then back again.

HOW TO READ PATTERNS

The Pokémon are mainly made in continuous rounds of stitches. At the beginning of each line you will find "RND" with the number of the round. But for some pieces you need to work in rows, where you turn your work to crochet the next row back. In this case the number of the row is indicated with "ROW."

At the end of each line, a number in brackets will show you the number of stitches you should have at the end of this round/row.

When you find the line "2 sc in each 4th sc," for example, it means you need to crochet one stitch (1 sc) in the first, second, and third stitch, and two stitches (2 sc) in the fourth stitch (4th sc), and repeat this until the end of the round.

This works in the same way for decreasing. When you find the line "dec over each 4th and 5th sc," it means you need to crochet one stitch (1 sc) in the first, second, and third stitch, and decrease over the next two stitches (2 sc) and repeat this, until the end of the round.

You may also find a line like this: "2 sc in the 1st, 2nd, 3rd sc." In this case you need to crochet two stitches (2 sc) in the indicated stitches, and crochet one stitch (1 sc) in the remaining stitches of the round. The following instruction should be read as, repeat the instructions between the two asterisks 3 times in total.

2 ch + 1 tch, turn around and crochet 2 sl.st 3x.

You must never skip a stitch and always finish the complete round unless specifically told otherwise.

BASIC STITCHES EXPLAINED

MAGIC RING

The Pokémon are mainly made in rounds. To start a round you usually use a technique called the magic ring. Until you get used to it, this can be a little bit fiddly as the yarn wants to twist away from you: just hold the yarn gently, but firmly and it will work.

1. Create a loop with the yarn by wrapping it over two fingers, then use your hook to pull the long length side of the yarn through the loop. (Like a big, loose stitch).

2. Don't pull it tight, you need to keep the ring big enough for your hook to work in and out of easily.

3. Wrap the long side of the yarn over the hook and pull it through the loop on your hook.

You have now completed the base of the magic ring. Continue on:

4. Insert the hook into the ring.

5. Wrap the long side of the yarn over your hook and pull it through the ring. You should have two loops around the hook.

6. Wrap the long side of the yarn over your hook and pull it through the two loops.

You have now completed the first single crochet in the magic ring.

7. Repeat Steps 4 to 7 until you have made the indicated amount of single crochet stitches into the ring. For most patterns you need to make six single crochet stitches into the ring.

8. Now pull carefully on the short side of the yarn to close the ring. You now have a filled disk of stitches.

1

5

2

6

3

7

4

8A

8B

CHAIN (CH)

Chain stitch is used in most patterns and is the basis of most crochet. If you need to work in rows, your first (base) row will be a series of chain stitches.

1. Create a loop with the yarn and use your hook to pull the long side of the yarn through the loop.

2. Pull the end to tighten the knot.

3. Wrap the long side of the yarn over your hook and pull it through the loop on your hook.

4. You have completed the first chain stitch.

5. Repeat Step 3.

6. Continue until you've made the indicated number of chain stitches you need for the pattern. In my patterns I also use the term "turning chain" (tch), this is the same as a normal chain stitch, but you do this at the end of a row. After you turn around your work, you skip this first stitch and continue with the second chain stitch from your hook.

SINGLE CROCHET (SC)

My Pokémon are primarily made using the single crochet stitch. To start, first make a magic ring or chain before you make a single crochet.

1. Insert the hook into the next stitch.

2. Wrap your yarn over the hook and pull it through the stitch. Now you should have two loops on your hook.

3. Wrap the yarn over the hook and pull it through both loops.

4. You have completed a single crochet, now continue with the next one.

SLIP STITCH (SL.ST)

All Pokémon patterns contain the slip stitch. This stitch is mainly used to tie off your crochet piece.

1. Insert your hook into the next stitch.

2. Wrap the yarn over the hook.

3. Pull it through the stitch and the loop on your hook.

4. Completed slip stitch.

INCREASE (2 SC IN 1 STITCH)

To increase, you crochet two single crochet stitches into one stitch.

1. Make a single crochet.

2. Continue working into the same stitch and crochet another single crochet. Now you have an extra stitch in your round (or row).

DECREASE WHILE CROCHETING IN ROUNDS (DEC)

This decreasing technique is only possible when you crochet in rounds.

1. Insert your hook into the front loop of the first stitch.

2. Insert your hook into the front loop of the second stitch.

3. Wrap the yarn over the hook and pull it through the two front loops. You should have two loops on your hook.

4. Wrap the yarn over the hook and pull it through the remaining loops. Now you have one stitch less in your round.

DECREASE WHILE CROCHETING IN ROWS OR BACK LOOPS (DEC)

When you crochet in rows, or when you need to crochet in the back loops only, you can't use the previous technique. Instead:

1. Insert your hook into the first stitch.

2. Wrap the yarn over the hook and pull it through the stitch. Now insert your hook in the second stitch, wrap the yarn over the hook and pull it through this stitch too. You should now have three loops on your hook.

3. Wrap the yarn over the hook and pull it through the three loops. Now you have one stitch less in your row.

DOUBLE CROCHET (DC)

A double crochet is bigger than a single crochet. To start a double crochet you often need to crochet a few chain stitches to gain height, but it's not always necessary.

1. Wrap the yarn over your hook and insert the hook through the next stitch.

2. Wrap the yarn over your hook and pull it through the stitch. You should now have three loops on your hook.

3. Wrap the yarn over the hook and pull it through the first two loops on your hook. You should have two loops remaining on your hook.

4. Wrap the yarn over your hook and pull it through the remaining two loops.

5. You have completed the double crochet.

HALF DOUBLE CROCHET (HDC)

The half double crochet is slightly smaller than a double crochet.

1. Wrap the yarn over the hook and insert it into the next stitch.

2. Wrap the yarn over the hook and pull it through the stitch. You should have three loops on your hook.

3. Wrap the yarn over the hook and pull it through all three loops on the hook.

4. You have completed the half double crochet.

CROCHET IN THE FRONT OR BACK LOOPS

Normally when you make a single crochet you go through the whole stitch—which means you go through both loops. Sometimes the pattern instructs you to crochet in the front (1) or back (2) loops only. This can be necessary to create an edge, for example.

SPECIAL TECHNIQUES

BIND OFF

You usually bind off (fasten off) with a slip stitch. For this, cut the remaining yarn, but leave a tail, usually enough to sew in later.

1. Crochet a slip stitch.

2. Pull on the loop until the entire yarn length is through it.

3. When you crochet in rows it is not always possible to bind off with a slip stitch. In this case you fasten off with an extra chain stitch.

4. Pull the cut yarn fully through the stitch.

COLOR SWITCH

To switch colors you start one stitch before it's indicated in the pattern, but it will only become visible from the next stitch.

1. Insert the hook into the next stitch.

2. Wrap the old color over your hook and pull it through the stitch.

3. You should have two loops on your hook.

4. Wrap the new color over your hook and pull it through both loops.

5. Cut the old color and tie the end to the short side of the new color on the inside of your work.

6. Continue with the new color.

STARTING A ROUND WITH A CHAIN

To create an oval piece you sometimes need to start with a chain instead of a magic ring.

1. Begin with as many chain stitches as instructed.

2. Turn around and crochet a single crochet in each chain stitch (unless told otherwise), don't forget to skip the turning chain.

3. Turn your work upside down to crochet into the other side of the chain stitches.

4. Crochet a single crochet in each chain stitch (unless told otherwise). Don't turn the work round, but continue working in spirals.

MAKING UP

CLOSING A PIECE

When you make a piece that needs to be closed at the end, you often end with six single crochet stitches. This leaves a small gap in your work.

1. To close a gap, crochet a slip stitch and cut the yarn, but leave sufficient tail to sew in later.

2. Attach the remaining yarn to a needle and go through the front loop of the first stitch.

3. Then go through the front loop of the next stitch.

4. Continue until you complete the round. Pull the yarn tight to minimize the gap.

5. Go through the center of the gap and finish on the other side of the piece.

6. Pull it tight and cut the remaining yarn.

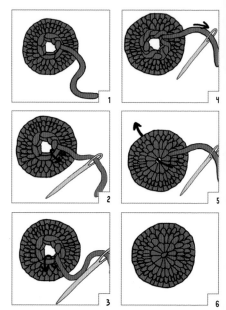

CROCHETING TWO PARTS TOGETHER

Sometimes you need to crochet multiple parts together. In the patterns, for example, the instruction is "crochet sc around the two parts."

1. Place the crochet pieces next to each other. Instead of crocheting in the next stitch of the current piece (b), insert your hook in a stitch of piece (a).

2. Crochet a single crochet and continue with that piece. When you've completed the round in piece (a), continue with the round you started with, ie. piece (b). Complete that round too. Sometimes it is necessary to skip a few stitches of a piece or to crochet the parts in a specific order. In this case it will be indicated in the pattern.

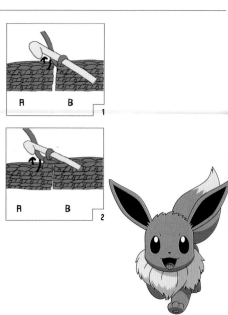

EMBROIDERY

Most of the Pokémon need some embroidery—to create a mouth for example.

1. Attach the yarn to a needle and go through a random stitch. Bring the yarn out where you want the mouth to begin.

2. Then go through the stitch where you want the mouth to end.

3. Bring the yarn out at the same stitch as the other yarn end—so where you started.

4. Tie the two yarn ends together and tuck the remaining yarn inside your piece.

If you need to make a curve, you can carefully put fabric glue between the yarn and your piece to create a shape.

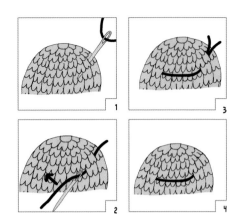

SEWING TWO PIECES TOGETHER

After you've made all the pieces for a character, you can start sewing them together. To decide the exact location for each part I recommend fixing all the pieces with pins first. To make this clear, I've made the pieces blue and red.

1. Thread the tail of the red piece through a needle. Take it through the first stitch of the blue piece where the red piece needs to be attached.

2. Push the needle from back to front through the next stitch of the red piece.

3. Go through the blue piece where you ended at Step 1 and come out on the other side of the next stitch.

4. Pull it tight. Repeat Steps 2 and 3 for all the stitches of the red piece.

After sewing the pieces together, go through the blue piece again, and let the yarn come out at a random place far from the red part. Cut the remaining yarn.

PiCHU

OFFICiAL COLORS

NATIONAL POKÉDEX NO.	TYPE	WEIGHT	HEIGHT
172	Electric	4.4 lb / 2.0 kg	1 ft / 0.3 m

Like many little ones, Pichu is full of energy—literally! When its cheek pouches are charged up with electricity, it runs and plays with no sign of tiring out. Unintentional shocks are a hazard of being this Pokémon's Trainer

MATERIALS

- Crochet hook 2.5mm

- 60 grams of yellow yarn (I used Phildar Phil Coton 3—Citron 1111)

- 20 grams of black yarn (I used Phildar Phil Coton 3—Noir 1200)

- Fiberfill

- Black, white, pink, and yellow felt

- Thin black yarn (I used Rico Essentials Crochet—12)

Finished size approximately
5$^1/_2$ inches (14 cm) high

TEMPLATES

Eyes

Cheeks

Fur Spikes

HEAD/BODY

(Use yellow yarn)

RND 1: 6 sc in magic ring (6)

RND 2: 2 sc in each sc (12)

RND 3: 2 sc in each 2nd sc (18)

RND 4: 2 sc in each 3rd sc (24)

RND 5: 2 sc in each 4th sc (30)

RND 6: 2 sc in each 5th sc (36)

RND 7: 2 sc in each 6th sc (42)

RND 8: 2 sc in each 7th sc (48)

RND 9: 2 sc in each 8th sc (54)

RND 10: 2 sc in each 9th sc (60)

RND 11-19: 60 sc (60)

RND 20: dec over each 9th and 10th sc (54)

RND 21: dec over each 8th and 9th sc (48)

RND 22: dec over each 7th and 8th sc (42)

RND 23: dec over each 6th and 7th sc (36)

RND 24: dec over each 5th and 6th sc (30)

RND 25: dec over each 4th and 5th sc (24)

RND 26: dec over each 3rd and 4th sc (18)

Start filling and keep filling until the last round.

RND 27: 2 sc in each 3rd sc (24)

RND 28: 2 sc in each 4th sc (30)

RND 29: 2 sc in each 5th sc (36)

RND 30: 36 sc (36)

RND 31: 2 sc in each 6th sc (42)

RND 32-37: 42 sc (42)

RND 38: dec over each 6th and 7th sc (36)

RND 39: dec over each 5th and 6th sc (30)

RND 40: dec over each 4th and 5th sc (24)

RND 41: dec over each 3rd and 4th sc (18)

RND 42: dec over each 2nd and 3rd sc (12)

RND 43: dec over each 2 sc (6)

Tie-off with a sl.st and close the head/body.

FEET (2x)

(Use yellow yarn)

RND 1: 6 sc in magic ring (6)

RND 2: 2 sc in each 3rd sc (8)

RND 3: 8 sc (8)

RND 4: 2 sc in each 4th sc (10)

RND 5-6: 10 sc (10)

RND 7: dec over each 4th and 5th sc (8)

RND 8: 8 sc (8)

RND 9: dec over each 3rd and 4th sc (6)

Tie-off with a sl.st and close the feet. Leave enough yarn for sewing.

ARMS (2x)

(Use yellow yarn)

RND 1: 6 sc in magic ring (6)

RND 2: 2 sc in each 3rd sc (8)

RND 3-4: 8 sc (8)

RND 5: 2 sc in each 4th sc (10)

RND 6-7: 10 sc (10)

RND 8: 2 sc in each 5th sc (12)

RND 9: 12 sc (12)

Fill the arms. Tie-off with a sl.st and leave enough yarn for sewing.

HEAD AND BODY

FOOT

ARM

COLLAR

(Use black yarn)

STEP 1. crochet 3 ch + 1 tch, turn around and crochet 1 sl.st in the 1st, 1 hdc in the 2nd, 1 dc in the 3rd ch,

STEP 2. crochet 1 ch,

STEP 3. crochet 3 ch + 1 tch, turn around and crochet 1 sl.st in the 1st, 1 hdc in the 2nd, 1 dc in the 3rd ch,

STEP 4. crochet 4 ch,

STEP 5. crochet 2 ch + 1 tch, turn around and crochet 1 sl.st in the 1st, 1 sc in the 2nd ch,

STEP 6. crochet 4 ch + 1 tch, turn around and crochet 1 sl.st in the 1st, 1 sc in the 2nd, 1 hdc in the 3rd, 1 dc in the 4th ch,

STEP 7. crochet 2 ch + 1 tch, turn around and crochet 1 sl.st in the 1st ch, 1 sc in the 2nd ch,

STEP 8. crochet 4 ch + 1 tch, turn around and crochet 1 sl.st in the 1st, 1 sc in the 2nd, 1 hdc in the 3rd, 1 dc in the 4th ch,

STEP 9. crochet 2 ch + 1 tch, turn around and crochet 1 sl.st in the 1st, 1 sc in the 2nd ch,

Step 10. crochet 4 ch

Tie-off and leave enough yarn for sewing.

TAIL (2X)

(Use black yarn)

ROW 1: 9 ch + 1 tch (9)

ROW 2-6: turn around and crochet 9 sc + 1 tch (9)

ROW 7: turn around and crochet 2 sc (don't crochet in the other 7 sc) + 1 tch (2)

ROW 8: turn around and crochet 2 sc + 1 tch (2)

ROW 9: turn around and dec over the 2 sc + 1 tch (1)

ROW 10: turn around and crochet 1 sc (1)

Tie-off (image a1).

Put the two tails facing each other and crochet them together with an edge of sc (image a2). Crochet 3 sc in the stitches at the corners to make them sharper.

Leave enough yarn for sewing (image a3).

COLLAR

EARS (4x)

(Make two in yellow and two in black)

ROW 1: 1 ch + 1 tch (1)

ROW 2: turn around and crochet 2 sc in the ch + 1 tch (2)

ROW 3: turn around and crochet 2 sc + 1 tch (2)

ROW 4: turn around and crochet 2 sc in the 1st, 2nd sc + 1 tch (4)

ROW 5: turn around and crochet 4 sc + 1 tch (4)

ROW 6: turn around and crochet 2 sc in the 1st, 4th sc + 1 tch (6)

ROW 7: turn around and crochet 6 sc + 1 tch (6)

ROW 8: turn around and crochet 2 sc in the 1st, 6th sc + 1 tch (8)

ROW 9: turn around and crochet 8 sc + 1 tch (8)

ROW 10: turn around and crochet 2 sc in the 1st, 8th sc + 1 tch (10)

ROW 11: turn around and crochet 10 sc + 1 tch (10)

ROW 12: turn around and crochet 2 sc in the 1st, 10th sc + 1 tch (12)

ROW 13: turn around and crochet 12 sc + 1 tch (12)

ROW 14: turn around and dec over the 1st and 2nd, 11th and 12th sc + 1 tch (10)

ROW 15: turn around and dec over the 1st and 2nd, 9th and 10th sc + 1 tch (8)

ROW 16: turn around and dec over the 1st and 2nd, 7th and 8th sc + 1 tch (6)

ROW 17: turn around and dec over the 1st and 2nd, 5th and 6th sc (4)

Tie-off and leave enough yarn for sewing.

EDGE OF THE EARS (2X)

(Use black yarn)

ROW 1: 28 ch + 1 tch (28)

ROW 2-3: turn around and crochet 28 sc + 1 tch (28)

ROW 4: turn around and crochet 14 sc, 2 ch + 1 tch, turn around and crochet 1 sl.st in the 1st ch, 1 sc in the 2nd ch, turn around to continue with the row and crochet 14 sc

Tie-off and leave enough yarn for sewing.

b1

b2

EAR EDGE

ASSEMBLY

Sew the feet to the bottom of the body.

To create the toes, make two stitch lines with yellow yarn on the front of the feet and pull them tight.

Sew the arms to the body, at round 28 to round 31.

Sew the tail to the body, at round 36 to round 37. To keep the tail up, you can sew it again at a higher point on the body.

Put the collar around the neck and sew the ends together.

Place a yellow ear on a black ear and sew them together (image b1). Sew the edge along the side of the ear. Note that the edge does not reach the bottom of the ear (image b2).

Sew the ears to the head, at round 6 to round 10.

Cut fur spikes out of yellow felt and glue these onto the back of the ears.

FACE

Cut two eyes out of black and white felt. Glue them onto the head at round 12 to round 17, with seven stitches between the eyes.

Embroider a nose on the head using thin black yarn, between rounds 17 and 18.

Embroider a mouth with thin black yarn to the head, at round 20.

Cut two cheeks out of pink felt and glue these onto the head, at round 18 to round 24.

WOBBUFFET

OFFICIAL COLORS

NATIONAL POKÉDEX NO.	TYPE	WEIGHT	HEIGHT
202	Psychic	62.8 lb / 28.5 kg	4ft 3 in / 1.3 m

Relying on its powers of endurance, Wobbuffet prefers not to attack—unless a foe goes after its tail. Then, it unleashes a powerful counterstrike..

MATERIALS

- Crochet hook 2.5mm

- 60 grams of blue yarn (I used Yarn and Colors Must-Have—Blue Lake 066)

- 10 grams of black yarn (I used Phildar Phil Coton 3—Noir 67)

- Fiberfill

- White felt

- Thin black yarn (I used Rico Essentials Crochet—12)

- Black textile marker

Finished size approximately
6 inches (15 cm) high

TEMPLATES

Eyes on tail

a1

a2

HEAD/BODY

(Use blue yarn)

RND 1: 6 sc in magic ring (6)

RND 2: 2 sc in each sc (12)

RND 3: 2 sc in each 2nd sc (18)

RND 4: 2 sc in each 3rd sc (24)

RND 5: 2 sc in each 4th sc (30)

RND 6: 2 sc in each 5th sc (36)

RND 7: 2 sc in each 6th sc (42)

RND 8: 2 sc in each 7th sc (48)

RND 9: 15 ch, skip the first 15 sc of the round and continue in the 16th sc (image a1), crochet 33 sc to finish the round (48)

RND 10: 2 sc in each 8th stitch (54)

RND 11: 2 sc in each 9th sc (60)

RND 12-24: 60 sc (60)

RND 25: dec over each 9th and 10th sc (54)

RND 26-27: 54 sc (54)

RND 28: dec over each 8th and 9th sc (48)

RND 29-30: 48 sc (48)

RND 31: dec over each 7th and 8th sc (42)

RND 32-33: 42 sc (42)

RND 34: dec over each 6th and 7th sc (36)

RND 35-36: 36 sc (36)

RND 37: dec over each 5th and 6th sc (30)

RND 38-39: 30 sc (30)

RND 40: dec over each 4th and 5th sc (24)

Start filling and keep filling until the last round.

RND 41-44: 24 sc (24)

RND 45: dec over each 3rd and 4th sc (18)

RND 46: dec over each 2nd and 3rd (12)

RND 47: dec over each 2 sc (6)

Tie-off with a sl.st and close the body (image a2).

BACK OF THE HEAD

(Use blue yarn)

Attach yarn to the open part of the head(images b1, b2).

RND 1: crochet 30 sc around the sc and ch (image b3) (30)

RND 2-9: 30 sc (30)

RND 10: dec over each 4th and 5th sc (24)

RND 11: 24 sc (24)

Start filling and keep filling slightly until the last round.

RND 12: dec over each 3rd and 4th sc (18)

RND 13: dec over each 2nd and 3rd sc (12)

RND 14: dec over each 2 sc (6)

Tie-off with a sl.st and close the back of the head. Let the yarn come out on the side of the piece and leave enough for sewing (image b4).

b1

b2

b3

b4

FEET (4x)

(Use blue yarn)

RND 1: 6 sc in magic ring (6)

RND 2: 2 sc in each sc (12)

RND 3: 2 sc in each 2nd sc (18)

RND 4-6: 18 sc (18)

RND 7: dec over each 2nd and 3rd sc (12)

RND 8-10: 12 sc (12)

Fill the feet. Tie-off with a sl.st and leave enough yarn for sewing.

ARMS (2x)

(Use blue yarn)

RND 1: 6 sc in magic ring (6)

RND 2: 2 sc in each sc (12)

RND 3: 12 sc in the back loops only (12)

RND 4-16: 12 sc, fill the arms until round 14 (12)

RND 17: dec over each 2 sc (6)

Tie-off with a sl.st and leave enough yarn for sewing.

TAIL

(Use black yarn)

RND 1: 6 sc in magic ring (6)

RND 2: 2 sc in the 1st, 2nd, 4th, 5th sc (10)

RND 3: 2 sc in the 1st, 2nd, 3rd, 4th, 6th, 7th, 8th, 9th sc (18)

RND 4-8: 18 sc (18)

RND 9: dec over each 5th and 6th sc (15)

RND 10: 15 sc (15)

RND 11: dec over each 4th and 5th sc (12)

RND 12: 12 sc (12)

RND 13: dec over each 3rd and 4th sc (9)

RND 14-15: 9 sc (9)

RND 16: dec over each 2nd and 3rd sc (6)

RND 17: 6 sc (6)

Tie-off with a sl.st and leave enough yarn for sewing.

FEET

ARMS

TAIL

ASSEMBLY

Use the remaining yarn on the back of the head to sew it closer to the head.

Sew the feet to the body, at round 43 to round 45.

Sew the arms to the body, with the top at round 24.

Sew the tail to the body, at round 39.

FACE

Embroider two eyes to the head with thin black yarn, at round 13 to round 15, with six stitches between the eyes. Work twice over the same spot, to make the eyes thicker.

Embroider a mouth to the head, with thin black yarn at round 18.

Cut two eyes out of white yarn. Glue these onto the tail, at round 5 to round 8, with two stitches between the eyes. Use a black textile marker to make the pupils.

EEVEE

OFFICIAL COLORS

NATIONAL POKÉDEX NO.	TYPE	WEIGHT	HEIGHT
133	Normal	14.3 lb / 6.5 kg	1 ft / 0.3 m

Because it can evolve into so many different Pokémon, researchers believe that Eevee's genes could help them figure out exactly how Pokémon Evolution works.

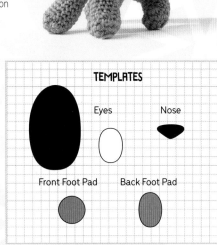

MATERIALS

- Crochet hook 2.5 mm
- 60 grams light brown yarn (I used SMC Catania—179)
- 25 grams off-white acrylic yarn (I used Stylecraft Special 4 ply—1005)
- 5 grams dark brown yarn (I used Phildar Phil Coton 3—Havane 1388)
- Fiberfill
- Black, white, and pink felt
- Thin black yarn (I used Durable Embroidery-crochet cotton—1001)
- Brush

Finished size approximately
6¼ inches (16 cm) high

TEMPLATES

Eyes

Nose

Front Foot Pad   Back Foot Pad

HEAD

(Use light brown yarn)

RND 1: 6 sc in magic ring (6)

RND 2: 2 sc in each sc (12)

RND 3: 2 sc in each 2nd sc (18)

RND 4: 2 sc in each 3rd sc (24)

RND 5: 2 sc in each 4th sc (30)

RND 6: 2 sc in each 5th sc (36)

RND 7: 2 sc in each 6th sc (42)

RND 8: 2 sc in each 14th sc (45)

RND 9–14: 45 sc (45)

RND 15: 2 sc in the 18th, 21st, 24th, 27th sc (49)

RND 16: 2 sc in the 19th, 23rd, 27th, 31st sc (53)

RND 17-19: 53 sc (53)

RND 20: dec over the 19th and 20th, 24th and 25th, 29th and 30th, 34th and 35th sc (49)

RND 21: dec over the 18th and 19th, 22nd and 23rd, 26th and 27th, 30th and 31st sc (45)

RND 22: dec over each 14th and 15th sc (42)

RND 23: dec over each 6th and 7th sc (36)

RND 24: dec over each 5th and 6th sc (30)

RND 25: dec over each 4th and 5th sc (24)

RND 26: dec over each 3rd and 4th sc (18)

Fill the head. Tie-off with a sl.st and leave enough yarn for sewing.

BODY

(Use light brown yarn)

RND 1: 6 sc in magic ring (6)

RND 2: 2 sc in each sc (12)

RND 3: 2 sc in each 2nd sc (18)

RND 4: 2 sc in each 3rd sc (24)

RND 5: 2 sc in each 4th sc (30)

RND 6: 2 sc in each 5th sc (36)

RND 7-24: 36 sc (36)

RND 25: dec over each 5th and 6th sc (30)

RND 26: dec over each 4th and 5th sc (24)

RND 27: dec over each 3rd and 4th sc (18)

Fill the body and keep filling until the last round.

RND 28: dec over each 2nd and 3rd sc (12)

RND 29: dec over each 2 sc (6)

Tie-off with a sl.st and close the body.

HEAD

BODY

FORELEGS (2X)

(Use light brown yarn)

RND 1: 6 sc in magic ring (6)

RND 2: 2 sc in each sc (12)

RND 3: 2 sc in the 1st, 2nd, 3rd, 4th sc (16)

RND 4: 16 sc (16)

RND 5: dec over the 1st and 2nd, 3rd and 4th, 5th and 6th, 7th and 8th sc (12)

RND 6-9: 12 sc (12)

RND 10: 2 sc in each 4th sc (15)

RND 11: 15 sc (15)

Fill the legs. Tie-off with a sl.st and leave enough yarn for sewing.

HIND LEGS (2X)

(Use light brown yarn)

RND 1: 6 sc in magic ring (6)

RND 2: 2 sc in each sc (12)

RND 3: 2 sc in the 1st, 2nd, 3rd, 4th sc (16)

RND 4: dec over the 1st and 2nd, 3rd and 4th, 5th and 6th, 7th and 8th sc, 2 sc in the 11th, 12th, 13th, 14th sc (16)

RND 5: dec over the 1st and 2nd, 3rd and 4th, 5th and 6th, 15th and 16th sc (12)

RND 6-9: 12 sc (12)

RND 10: 2 sc in each 2nd sc (18)

RND 11-12: 18 sc (18)

Fill the legs. Tie-off with a sl.st and leave enough yarn for sewing.

TAIL

(Start with off-white acrylic yarn)

RND 1: 6 sc in magic ring (6)

RND 2: 6 sc (6)

RND 3: 2 sc in each sc (12)

RND 4-5: 12 sc (12)

RND 6: 2 sc in each 2nd sc (18)

RND 7-8: 18 sc (18)

RND 9: 2 sc in each 3rd sc (24)

RND 10: 24 sc (24)

RND 11: 2 sc in each 4th sc (30)

RND 12: 30 sc (30)

RND 13: 2 sc in each 5th sc (36)

(Switch to light brown yarn)

RND 14: 36 sc (36)

RND 15: 2 sc in each 6th sc (42)

RND 16-26: 42 sc (42)

RND 27: dec over each 6th and 7th sc (36)

RND 28: 36 sc (36)

RND 29: dec over each 5th and 6th sc (30)

RND 30: 30 sc (30)

RND 31: dec over each 4th and 5th sc (24)

RND 32: dec over each 3rd and 4th sc (18)

Fill the tail. Tie-off with a sl.st and leave enough yarn for sewing. Brush the end of the tail out to make it fluffy.

FORELEG

HIND LEG

TAIL

OUTER EARS (2x)

(Use light brown yarn)

RND 1: 4 sc in magic ring (4)

RND 2: 4 sc (4)

RND 3: 2 sc in each sc (8)

RND 4: 8 sc (8)

RND 5: 2 sc in each 4th sc (10)

RND 6: 10 sc (10)

RND 7: 2 sc in each 5th sc (12)

RND 8: 12 sc (12)

RND 9: 2 sc in each 4th sc (15)

RND 10-11: 15 sc (15)

RND 12: 2 sc in each 5th sc (18)

RND 13-15: 18 sc (18)

RND 16: dec over each 5th and 6th sc (15)

RND 17-18: 15 sc (15)

RND 19: dec over each 4th and 5th sc (12)

RND 20: 12 sc (12)

Tie-off with a sl.st and leave enough yarn for sewing.

INNER EARS (2x)

(Use dark brown yarn)

ROW 1: 14 ch + 1 tch (14)

ROW 2: turn around and crochet 1 sl.st, 2 sc, 8 hdc, 2 sc, 1 sl.st, continue on the other side of the chain, crochet 1 sl.st, 2 sc, 8 hdc, 2 sc, 1 sl.st

Tie-off and leave enough yarn for sewing.

OUTER EAR   **INNER EAR**

a1

a2

a3

a4

ASSEMBLY

Sew the head to the body, at round 6 to round 12.

Sew the legs to the body. Sew the forelegs at round 6 to round 10, and the hind legs at round 18 to round 23.

To create the toes, make two stitch lines with light brown yarn on the front of the feet, and pull them tight.

Cut four paw pads out of pink felt. Glue them to the bottom of the legs.

Sew the tail to the back of the body.

Sew the inner ears to the outer ears. Then sew the ears to the head, at round 7 to round 11.

COLLAR

Attach pieces of off-white acrylic yarn to the body (images a1–a4).

Make about four rows around the body below the head.

Brush the yarn out to make it fluffy.

FACE

Cut two eyes out of black and white felt. Glue them onto the head, at round 10 to round 16, with six stitches between the eyes.

Cut a nose out of black felt. Glue it onto the head, at round 16.

Embroider a mouth to the head with thin black yarn, at round 18.

Embroider two eyebrows to the head with thin black yarn, at round 9.

PiKACHU

OFFICIAL COLORS

NATIONAL POKÉDEX No.	TYPE	WEIGHT	HEIGHT
25	Electric	13.2 lb / 6.0 kg	1ft 4 in / 0.4 m

If you come across a Pikachu in its forest home, watch out for its red cheeks! That's where it stores electricity, so if you touch them, you'll get zapped.

MATERIALS

- Crochet hook 2.5 mm

- 70 grams of yellow yarn (I used Yarn and Colors Must-Have—013)

- 5 grams of black yarn (I used Phildar Phil Coton 3—Noir 1200)

- 10 grams of brown yarn (I used Phildar Phil Coton 3—Havane 1388)

- Fiberfill

- Black, white, and red felt

- Thin black yarn (I used Rico Essentials Crochet—12)

Finished size approximately 6¹/₂ inches (17 cm) high

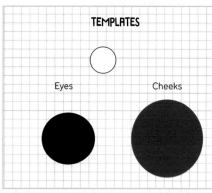

TEMPLATES

Eyes

Cheeks

HEAD/BODY

(Use yellow yarn)

RND 1: 6 sc in magic ring (6)

RND 2: 2 sc in each sc (12)

RND 3: 2 sc in each 2nd sc (18)

RND 4: 2 sc in each 3rd sc (24)

RND 5: 2 sc in each 4th sc (30)

RND 6: 2 sc in each 5th sc (36)

RND 7: 2 sc in each 6th sc (42)

RND 8: 2 sc in each 7th sc (48)

RND 9: 2 sc in each 8th sc (54)

RND 10-17: 54 sc (54)

RND 18: 2 sc in the 6th, 10th, 14th, 18th, 22nd, 26th sc (60)

RND 19-21: 60 sc (60)

RND 22: dec over the 6th and 7th, 11th and 12th, 16th and 17th, 21st and 22nd, 26th and 27th, 31st and 32nd sc (54)

RND 23: dec over each 8th and 9th sc (48)

RND 24: dec over each 7th and 8th sc (42)

RND 25: 2 sc in each 7th sc (48)

RND 26: 48 sc (48)

RND 27: 2 sc in the 3rd, 9th, 27th, 33rd, 39th, 45th sc (54)

RND 28: 54 sc (54)

RND 29: 2 sc in each 9th sc (60)

RND 30: 60 sc (60)

RND 31: 2 sc in the 3rd, 10th, 35th, 42nd, 49th, 56th sc (66)

RND 32-40: 66 sc (66)

RND 41: dec over the 4th and 5th, 12th and 13th, 15th and 16th, 18th and 19th, 21st and 22nd, 30th and 31st, 33rd and 34th, 36th and 37th, 38th and 39th, 46th and 47th, 54th and 55th, 62nd and 63rd sc (54)

Start filling and keep filling until the last round.

RND 42: dec over each 8th and 9th sc (48)

RND 43: dec over each 7th and 8th sc (42)

RND 44: dec over each 6th and 7th sc (36)

RND 45: dec over each 5th and 6th sc (30)

RND 46: dec over each 4th and 5th sc (24)

RND 47: dec over each 3rd and 4th sc (18)

RND 48: dec over each 2nd and 3rd sc (12)

RND 49: dec over each 2 sc (6)

Tie-off with a sl.st and close the body.

EARS (2X)

(Start with black yarn)

RND 1: 6 sc in magic ring (6)

RND 2: 6 sc (6)

RND 3: 2 sc in each 2nd sc (9)

RND 4: 9 sc (9)

RND 5: 2 sc in each 3rd sc (12)

RND 6: 2 sc in each 4th sc (15)

(In the next rounds you switch between yellow and black yarn)

RND 7: 3 sc in yellow, 10 sc in black, 2 sc in yellow (15)

RND 8: 5 sc in yellow, 6 sc in black, 4 sc in yellow (15)

RND 9: 7 sc in yellow, 2 sc in black, 6 sc in yellow (15)

(Continue with yellow yarn)

RND 10-18: 15 sc (15)

RND 19: dec over each 4th and 5th sc (12)

RND 20: 12 sc (12)

Fill the ears. Tie-off with a sl.st and leave enough yarn for sewing.

HEAD/BODY

Back   Front

EARS

FEET (2x)

(Use yellow yarn)

RND 1: 6 sc in magic ring (6)

RND 2: 2 sc in each 2nd sc (9)

RND 3: 9 sc (9)

RND 4: 2 sc in each 3rd sc (12)

RND 5: 12 sc (12)

RND 6: 2 sc in each 4th sc (15)

RND 7-9: 15 sc (15)

RND 10: dec over each 4th and 5th sc (12)

RND 11: dec over each 2 sc (6)

Tie-off with a sl.st and close the feet. Let the yarn come out on the top of the feet and leave enough for sewing.

ARMS (2x)

(Use yellow yarn)

RND 1: 6 sc in magic ring (6)

RND 2: 2 sc in each sc (12)

RND 3-4: 12 sc (12)

RND 5: 2 sc in each 4th sc (15)

RND 6-9: 15 sc (15)

RND 10: dec over each 4th and 5th sc (12)

RND 11: 12 sc (12)

RND 12: dec over each 3rd and 4th sc (9)

RND 13: 9 sc (9)

RND 14: dec over each 2nd and 3rd sc (6)

Tie-off with a sl.st and close the arms. Let the yarn come out on the side of the arms and leave enough for sewing.

STRiPES (2x)

(Use brown yarn)

ROW 1: 16 ch + 1 tch (16)

ROW 2: turn around and crochet 16 sc (16)

Tie-off with a sl.st and leave enough yarn for sewing.

TAIL (2x)

(Start with yellow yarn)

ROW 1: 15 ch + 1 tch (15)

ROW 2: turn around and crochet 15 sc + 1 tch (15)

ROW 3: turn around and dec over the 14th and 15th sc + 1 tch (14)

ROW 4: turn around and crochet 14 sc + 1 tch (14)

ROW 5: turn around and dec over the 13th and 14th sc + 1 tch (13)

ROW 6: turn around and crochet 13 sc + 1 tch (13)

ROW 7: turn around and dec over the 12th and 13th sc + 1 tch (12)

ROW 8: turn around and crochet 12 sc + 1 tch (12)

ROW 9: turn around and crochet 5 sc (don't crochet in the other 7 sc) + 1 tch (5)

ROW 10-11: turn around and crochet 5 sc + 1 tch (5)

ROW 12: turn around and crochet 5 sc and 4 ch + 1 tch (9)

ROW 13-16: turn around and crochet 9 sc + 1 tch (9)

a1

a2

FEET   ARM   STRiPE   TAIL

ROW 17: turn around and crochet 4 sc (don't crochet in the other 5 sc) + 1 tch (4)

(In the next round you switch between yellow and brown yarn)

ROW 18: 1 sc in yellow, 1 sc in brown, 1 sc in yellow, 1 sc in brown (4)

(Continue with brown yarn)

ROW 19: turn around and crochet 4 sc + 1 tch (4)

ROW 20: turn around and crochet 4 sc and 3 ch + 1 tch (7)

ROW 21: turn around and crochet 7 sc + 1 tch (7)

ROW 22: turn around and crochet 7 sc (7)

Tie-off (image a1).

Put the two tails on top of each other. Crochet them together with an edge of sc. Crochet 3 sc in the stitches at the corners for more sharpness (image a2).

Leave enough yarn for sewing.

ASSEMBLY

Sew the ears to the head, at round 8 to round 11.

Sew the arms at right angles to the body, starting at round 27.

To create the fingers, make two stitch lines with yellow yarn on the end of the arms and pull them tight.

Sew the feet to the bottom of the body. To create the toes, make two stitch lines with yellow yarn on the front of the feet, and pull them tight.

Sew the stripes to the back. Sew the first stripe at round 29 and the second stripe about round 34.

Sew the tail to the body at round 40. To keep the tail up, attach it at another higher point on the body as well.

FACE

Cut two eyes out of black and white felt. Glue them onto the head, at round 12 to round 16, with seven stitches between the eyes.

Sew a cute little nose with thin black yarn, at round 16.

Split a piece of the black yarn to make it thinner and use it to sew a mouth to the head, at round 19.

Cut two cheeks out of red felt. Glue these onto the head, at round 17 to round 22.

MEOWTH

OFFICIAL COLORS

NATIONAL POKÉDEX NO.	TYPE	WEIGHT	HEIGHT
52	Normal	9.3 lb / 4.2 kg	1ft 4 in / 0.4 m

Meowth tends to sleep during the day and becomes more active after dark. When something shiny and round catches this Pokémon's eye, it immediately gets added to Meowth's collection.

MATERIALS

- Crochet hook 2.5mm

- 70 grams of cream yarn (I used SMC Catania—404)

- 15 grams of brown yarn (I used SMC Catania—383)

- 5 grams of pink yarn (I used Phildar Phil Coton 3—Berlingot 1198)

- 5 grams of gold yarn (I used Phildar Phil Coton 3—Gold 1233)

- Fiberfill

- Metal wire or pipe cleaner *

- Black, white, and pink felt

- Thin black yarn (I used Rico Essentials Crochet—12)

Finished size approximately
6¼ inches (16 cm) high

TEMPLATES

Eyes

Teeth

Paw pads

Toe pad

Heel pad

Ear edges

HEAD/BODY

(Use cream yarn)

RND 1: 6 sc in magic ring (6)

RND 2: 2 sc in each sc (12)

RND 3: 2 sc in each 2nd sc (18)

RND 4: 2 sc in each 3rd sc (24)

RND 5: 2 sc in each 4th sc (30)

RND 6: 2 sc in each 5th sc (36)

RND 7: 2 sc in each 6th sc (42)

RND 8: 2 sc in each 7th sc (48)

RND 9: 2 sc in each 8th sc (54)

RND 10: 2 sc in each 9th sc (60)

RND 11: 60 sc (60)

RND 12: 2 sc in each 10th sc (66)

RND 13-20: 66 sc (66)

RND 21: dec over each 10th and 11th sc (60)

RND 22: dec over each 9th and 10th sc (54)

RND 23: dec over each 8th and 9th sc (48)

RND 24: dec over each 7th and 8th sc (42)

RND 25: dec over each 6th and 7th sc (36)

RND 26: dec over each 5th and 6th sc (30)

RND 27: dec over each 4th and 5th sc (24)

RND 28: dec over each 3rd and 4th sc (18)

Start filling and keep filling until the last round.

RND 29: 2 sc in each 3rd sc (24)

RND 30: 2 sc in each 4th sc (30)

RND 31: 30 sc (30)

RND 32: 2 sc in each 5th sc (36)

RND 33-40: 36 sc (36)

RND 41: dec over each 5th and 6th sc (30)

RND 42: dec over each 4th and 5th sc (24)

RND 43: dec over each 3rd and 4th sc (18)

RND 44: dec over each 2nd and 3rd sc (12)

RND 45: dec over each 2 sc (6)

Tie-off with a sl.st and close the head/body.

a1

a2

FINGERS (6X)

(Use cream yarn)

RND 1: 4 sc in magic ring (4)

RND 2: 4 sc (4)

Tie-off four fingers with a sl.st, leave a small piece of yarn for sewing. Do not tie-off two fingers. Continue with the arms.

HEAD AND BODY

FINGER

ARMS (2X)

(Use cream yarn)

In the next round you will join three fingers to create the arms.

RND 3: lay three fingers next to each other with the finger that you didn't tie-off on the right,

STEP 1. go to the middle finger and crochet 2 sc, (image a1)

STEP 2. go to the left finger and crochet 4sc,(image a2)

STEP 3. continue with the middle finger and crochet 2 sc,

STEP 4. go to the right finger and crochet 4 sc (12),

RND 4: dec over each 2nd and 3rd sc (8)

Start filling and keep filling until round 13. Don't fill the rounds after.

RND 5-13: 8 sc (8)

RND 14: dec over each 3rd and 4th sc (6)

RND 15-16: 6 sc (6)

Tie-off with a sl.st and leave enough yarn for sewing.

TOES (6X)

(Use brown yarn)

RND 1: 4 sc in magic ring (4)

RND 2: 4 sc (4)

Tie-off four toes with a sl.st, leave a small piece of yarn for sewing. Do not tie-off two toes. Continue with the feet.

FEET (2X)

In the next round you will join three toes to create the foot.

RND 3: lay three toes next to each other with the toe that you didn't tie-off on the right,

STEP 1. go to the middle toe and crochet 2 sc,

STEP 2. go to the left toe and crochet 4 sc,

STEP 3. continue with the middle toe and crochet 2 sc,

STEP 4. go to the right toe and crochet 4 sc (12)

RND 4: 12 sc (12)

RND 5: dec over each 3rd and 4th sc (9)

RND 6-7: 9 sc (9)

(Switch to cream yarn)

RND 8-11: 9 sc (9)

RND 12: dec over each 2nd and 3rd sc (6)

Tie-off with a sl.st and close the feet.

LEGS (2X)

(Use cream yarn)

Leave enough yarn at the beginning for sewing.

RND 1: 7 ch and finish with a sl.st in the 1st ch to connect the chain (7)

RND 2-8: 7 sc (7)

Tie-off with a sl.st and leave enough yarn for sewing. Place a piece of metal wire or a pipe cleaner inside the legs to bend them.

TAIL (2X)

(Start with brown yarn)

RND 1: 6 sc in magic ring (6)

RND 2: 2 sc in each 2nd sc (9)

RND 3-21: 9 sc, fill the tail slightly until round 21, don't fill the rounds after (9)

RND 22: dec over each 2nd and 3rd sc (6)

RND 23: 6 sc (6)

(Switch to cream yarn)

RND 24-36: 6 sc (6)

Tie-off with a sl.st and leave enough yarn for sewing. Place a piece of metal wire or a pipe cleaner inside the tail to bend it. To keep the curl at the beginning of the tail you can use (fabric) glue.

FINISHED ARM

FOOT **LEG** **TAIL**

OUTER EARS (2x)

(Use cream yarn)

RND 1: 6 sc in magic ring (6)

RND 2: 6 sc (6)

RND 3: 2 sc in each sc (12)

RND 4: 12 sc (12)

RND 5: 2 sc in each 2nd sc (18)

RND 6: 18 sc (18)

RND 7: 2 sc in each 3rd sc (24)

RND 8: 24 sc (24)

RND 9: 2 sc in each 4th sc (30)

RND 10-11: 30 sc (30)

Fill the ears slightly. Tie-off with a sl.st and leave enough yarn for sewing.

INNER EARS (2x)

(Use pink yarn)

ROW 1: 1 ch + 1 tch (1)

ROW 2: turn around and crochet 2 sc in the ch + 1 tch (2)

ROW 3: turn around and crochet 2 sc in the 1st, 2nd sc + 1 tch (4)

ROW 4: turn around and crochet 4 sc + 1 tch (4)

ROW 5: turn around and crochet 2 sc in the 1st, 4th sc + 1 tch (6)

ROW 6: turn around and crochet 2 sc in the 1st, 6th sc + 1 tch (8)

ROW 7: turn around and crochet 8 sc (8)

Tie-off and leave enough yarn for sewing.

AMULET (2x)

(Use gold yarn)

RND 1: 8 ch + 1 tch (8)

RND 2: turn around and crochet 8 sc, continue on the other side of the row and crochet 8 sc (16)

Don't turn around, but continue crocheting in rounds.

RND 3: 2 sc in the 1st, 8th, 9th, 16th sc (20)

Tie-off with a sl.st and leave enough yarn for sewing.

OUTER EAR

INNER EAR

EAR ASSEMBLY

AMULET

HAIR (2x)

(Use cream yarn)

ROW 1: 10 ch + 1 tch (10)

ROW 2: turn around and crochet 10 sl.st (10)

Tie-off and leave enough yarn for sewing.

WHISKERS (4x)

(Use cream yarn)

ROW 1: 11 ch + 1 tch (11)

ROW 2: turn around and crochet 11 sl.st (11)

Tie-off and leave enough yarn for sewing.

WHISKER

ASSEMBLY

Sew the arms to the body, at round 29.

Sew the legs to the feet, at rounds 10 to 11. Then sew the other side of the legs to the body, at rounds 42 to 43.

Cut six round and two oval paw pads out of pink felt. Glue them on the bottom of the feet.

Sew the tail to the body, at rounds 39 to 40.

Sew the inner ears to the outer ears. Then sew the ears to the head, at round 4 to round 14.

Cut the edges of the ears out of black felt. Glue them on the front of the ears.

Lay the two amulet parts on each other and sew them together. On the front, embroider four horizontal lines with thin black yarn.

Sew the amulet to the head, with the bottom at round 12.

Sew the hair to the head, between rounds 6 and 7.

Sew the whiskers to the head, at round 16 and round 20.

FACE

Cut two eyes out of white and black felt.

Glue them onto the head, at round 13 to round 18, with six stitches between the eyes.

Embroider a mouth on the head with thin black yarn, at rounds 20 to 21.

Cut two teeth out of white felt. Glue them onto the head below the mouth.

JOLTEON

OFFICIAL COLORS

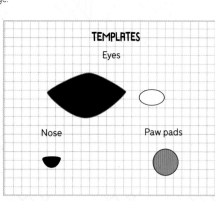

NATIONAL POKÉDEX NO.	TYPE	WEIGHT	HEIGHT
135	Electric	54.0 lb / 24.5 kg	2 ft 7 in / 0.8 m

Jolteon's mood shifts as fast as lightning—one moment it's joyous, the next it's furious. These shifting emotions somehow increase its electrical charge.

MATERIALS

- Crochet hook 2.5mm
- 80 grams of yellow yarn (I used Phildar Phil Coton 3—Soleil 1440)
- 5 grams of black yarn (I used Phildar Phil Coton 3—Noir 1200)
- 5 grams of white yarn (I used Phildar Phil Coton 3—Blanc 1225)
- Thin black yarn (I used Rico Essentials Crochet—12)
- Fiberfill
- Black, white, and pink felt

Finished size approximately
7 inches (18 cm) high

TEMPLATES

Eyes

Nose

Paw pads

HEAD

(Use yellow yarn)

RND 1: 6 sc in magic ring (6)

RND 2: 2 sc in each sc (12)

RND 3: 2 sc in each 2nd sc (18)

RND 4: 2 sc in each 3rd sc (24)

RND 5: 2 sc in each 4th sc (30)

RND 6: 2 sc in each 5th sc (36)

RND 7: 2 sc in each 6th sc (42)

RND 8: 2 sc in each 7th sc (48)

RND 9-14: 48 sc (48)

RND 15: 2 sc in the 21st, 24th, 27th, 30th sc (52)

RND 16: 2 sc in the 22nd, 26th, 30th, 34th sc (56)

RND 17-19: 56 sc (56)

RND 20: dec over the 22nd and 23rd, 27th and 28th, 32nd and 33rd, 37th and 38th sc (52)

RND 21: dec over the 21st and 22nd, 25th and 26th, 29th and 30th, 33rd and 34th sc (48)

RND 22: dec over each 7th and 8th sc (42)

RND 23: dec over each 6th and 7th sc (36)

RND 24: dec over each 5th and 6th sc (30)

RND 25: dec over each 4th and 5th sc (24)

RND 26: dec over each 3rd and 4th sc (18)

Fill the head. Tie-off with a sl.st and leave enough yarn for sewing.

BODY

(Use yellow yarn)

RND 1: 6 sc in magic ring (6)

RND 2: 2 sc in each sc (12)

RND 3: 2 sc in each 2nd sc (18)

RND 4: 2 sc in each 3rd sc (24)

RND 5: 2 sc in each 4th sc (30)

RND 6: 2 sc in each 5th sc (36)

RND 7: 2 sc in each 12th sc (39)

RND 8-26: 39 sc (39)

RND 27: dec over each 12th and 13th sc (36)

RND 28: dec over each 5th and 6th sc (30)

RND 29: dec over each 4th and 5th sc (24)

Fill the body and keep filling until the last round.

RND 30: dec over each 3rd and 4th sc (18)

RND 31: dec over each 2nd and 3rd sc (12)

RND 32: dec over each 2 sc (6)

Tie-off with a sl.st and close the body.

FORELEGS (2X)

(Use yellow yarn)

RND 1: 6 sc in magic ring (6)

RND 2: 2 sc in each sc (12)

RND 3: 2 sc in the 1st, 2nd, 3rd, 4th sc (16)

RND 4: 16 sc (16)

RND 5: dec over the 1st and 2nd, 3rd and 4th, 5th and 6th, 7th and 8th sc (12)

RND 6-10: 12 sc (12)

RND 11: 2 sc in each 4th sc (15)

RND 12: 15 sc (15)

Fill the legs. Tie-off with a sl.st and leave enough yarn for sewing.

HIND LEGS (2X)

(Use yellow yarn)

RND 1: 6 sc in magic ring (6)

RND 2: 2 sc in each sc (12)

RND 3: 2 sc in the 1st, 2nd, 3rd, 4th sc (16)

RND 4: dec over the 1st and 2nd, 3rd and 4th, 5th and 6th, 7th and 8th sc, 2 sc in the 11th, 12th, 13th, 14th sc (16)

RND 5: dec over the 1st and 2nd, 3rd and 4th, 5th and 6th, 15th and 16th sc (12)

RND 6-9: 12 sc (12)

RND 10: 2 sc in each 2nd sc (18)

RND 11-13: 18 sc (18)

Fill the legs. Tie-off with a sl.st and leave enough yarn for sewing.

BODY

HEAD

FORELEGS

HIND LEGS

BACK SPIKES

PART 1

(Use yellow yarn)

RND 1: 4 sc in magic ring (4)

RND 2: 4 sc (4)

RND 3: 2 sc in each 2nd sc (6)

RND 4: 6 sc (6)

RND 5: 2 sc in each 3rd sc (8)

RND 6: 8 sc (8)

RND 7: 2 sc in each 4th sc (10)

RND 8: 10 sc (10)

Tie-off with a sl.st.

PART 2

(Use yellow yarn)

RND 1: 4 sc in magic ring (4)

RND 2: 4 sc (4)

RND 3: 2 sc in each 2nd sc (6)

RND 4: 6 sc (6)

RND 5: 2 sc in each 3rd sc (8)

Tie-off with a sl.st.

PART 3

(Use yellow yarn)

RND 1: 4 sc in magic ring (4)

RND 2: 4 sc (4)

RND 3: 2 sc in each 2nd sc (6)

RND 4: 6 sc (6)

RND 5: 2 sc in each 3rd sc (8)

RND 6: 8 sc (8)

RND 7: 2 sc in each 4th sc (10)

RND 8: 10 sc (10)

Tie-off with a sl.st.

PART 4

(Use yellow yarn)

RND 1: 4 sc in magic ring (4)

RND 2: 4 sc (4)

RND 3: 2 sc in each 2nd sc (6)

RND 4: 6 sc (6)

RND 5: 2 sc in each 3rd sc (8)

RND 6: 8 sc (8)

RND 7: 2 sc in each 4th sc (10)

RND 8: 10 sc (10)

RND 9: 2 sc in each 5th sc (12)

RND 10: 12 sc (12)

RND 11: 2 sc in each 6th sc (14)

RND 12: 14 sc (14)

RND 13: crochet around parts one–four (image a1):

  STEP 1. first crochet 5 sc of part one,

  STEP 2. continue with part two and crochet 4 sc (image a2),

  STEP 3. continue with part three, and crochet 10 sc (image a3),

  STEP 4. continue with part two and crochet 4 sc,

  STEP 5. continue with part one and crochet 5 sc,

  STEP 6. continue with part four and crochet 14 sc (42)

RND 14: 42 sc (42)

RND 15: dec over each 6th and 7th sc (36)

Tie-off with a sl.st (image a4)

PART 5

(Use yellow yarn)

RND 1: 4 sc in magic ring (4)

RND 2: 4 sc (4)

RND 3: 2 sc in each 2nd sc (6)

RND 4: 6 sc (6)

RND 5: 2 sc in each 3rd sc (8)

RND 6: 8 sc (8)

RND 7: 2 sc in each 4th sc (10)

RND 8: 10 sc (10)

Tie-off with a sl.st.

a1

a2

a3

a4

a5

PART 6

(Use yellow yarn)

RND 1: 4 sc in magic ring (4)

RND 2: 4 sc (4)

RND 3: 2 sc in each 2nd sc (6)

RND 4: 6 sc (6)

RND 5: 2 sc in each 3rd sc (8)

Tie-off with a sl.st.

PART 7

(Use yellow yarn)

RND 1: 4 sc in magic ring (4)

RND 2: 4 sc (4)

RND 3: 2 sc in each 2nd sc (6)

RND 4: 6 sc (6)

RND 5: 2 sc in each 3rd sc (8)

RND 6: 8 sc (8)

RND 7: 2 sc in each 4th sc (10)

RND 8: 10 sc (10)

Tie-off with a sl.st.

PART 8

(Use yellow yarn)

RND 1: 4 sc in magic ring (4)

RND 2: 4 sc (4)

RND 3: 2 sc in each 2nd sc (6)

RND 4: 6 sc (6)

RND 5: 2 sc in each 3rd sc (8)

RND 6: 8 sc (8)

RND 7: 2 sc in each 4th sc (10)

RND 8: 10 sc (10)

RND 9: 2 sc in each 5th sc (12)

RND 10: 12 sc (12)

RND 11: 2 sc in each 6th sc (14)

RND 12: 14 sc (14)

RND 13: crochet around part 5-8:

   STEP 1. first crochet 5 sc of part five,

   STEP 2. continue with part five and crochet 4 sc,

   STEP 3. continue with part seven and crochet 10 sc,

   STEP 4. continue with part six and crochet 4 sc,

   STEP 5. continue with part five and crochet 5 sc,

   STEP 6. continue with part eight and crochet 14 sc (42)

RND 14: 42 sc (42)

RND 15: dec over each 6th and 7th sc (36)

RND 16: crochet around part four and eight (image a5),

   STEP 1. first crochet 31 sc of part eight,

   STEP 2. continue with part four and crochet 36 sc (make sure that the big point will be next to each other)

   STEP 3. continue with part eight and crochet the other 5 sc (72)

RND 17: 72 sc (72)

RND 18: dec over each 5th and 6th sc (60)

RND 19-20: 60 sc (60)

RND 21: dec over each 4th and 5th sc (48)

RND 22: 48 sc (48)

Tie-off with a sl.st and leave enough yarn for sewing.

CHEEKS (2x)

(Use yellow yarn)

   STEP 1. crochet 3 ch + 1 tch, turn around and crochet 1 sl.st in the 1st ch, 1 sc in the 2nd-3rd ch,

   STEP 2. crochet 5 ch + 1 tch, turn around and crochet 1 sl.st in the 1st ch, 1 sc in the 2nd ch, 1 hdc in the 3rd-4th ch, don't crochet in the 5th ch,

   STEP 3. crochet 5 ch + 1 tch, turn around and crochet 1 sl.st in the 1st ch, 1 sc in the 2nd ch, 1 hdc in the 3rd-4th ch, don't crochet in the 5th ch,

   STEP 4. crochet 4 ch + 1 tch, turn around and crochet 1 sl.st in the 1st ch, 1 sc in the 2nd-3rd ch, don't crochet in the 4th ch

Tie-off and leave enough yarn for sewing.

SPIKES BACK

SPIKES CHEEKS

COLLAR

(Use white yarn)

ROW 1: 30 ch + 1 tch (30)

ROW 2-3: turn around and crochet 30 sc + 1 tch (30)

ROW 4: turn around and crochet 8 ch + 1 tch, turn around and crochet 1 sl.st in the 1st ch, 1 sc in the 2nd ch, 1 hdc in the 3rd ch, 1 dc in the 4th-8th ch, finish with a sl.st in the 3rd sc of the row (so you skip 2 sc),

STEP 1. crochet 4 ch + 1 tch, turn around and crochet 1 sl.st in the 1st ch, 1 sc in the 2nd ch, 1 hdc in the 3rd-4th ch, finish with a sl.st in the 5th sc of the round (so you skip 1 sc),

STEP 2. crochet 8 ch + 1 tch, turn around and crochet 1 sl.st in the 1st ch, 1 sc in the 2nd ch, 1 hdc in the 3rd ch, 1 dc in the 4th-8th ch, finish with a sl.st in the 8th sc of the round (so you skip 2 sc),

STEP 3. crochet 5 ch + 1 tch, turn around and crochet 1 sl.st in the 1st ch, 1 sc in the 2nd ch, 1 hdc in the 3rd-5th ch, finish with a sl.st in the 10th sc of the round (so you skip 1 sc),

STEP 4. crochet 7 ch + 1 tch, turn around and crochet 1 sl.st in the 1st ch, 1 sc in the 2nd ch, 1 hdc in the 3rd ch, 1 dc in the 4th-7th ch, finish with a sl.st in the 13th sc of the round (so you skip 2 sc),

STEP 5. crochet 8 ch + 1 tch, turn around and crochet 1 sl.st in the 1st ch, 1 sc in the 2nd ch, 1 hdc in the 3rd ch, 1 dc in the 4th-8th ch, finish with a sl.st in the 16th sc of the round (so you skip 2 sc),

STEP 6. crochet 4 ch + 1 tch, turn around and crochet 1 sl.st in the 1st ch, 1 sc in the 2nd ch, 1 hdc in the 3rd-4th ch, finish with a sl.st in the 18th sc of the round (so you skip 1 sc),

STEP 7. crochet 6 ch + 1 tch, turn around and crochet 1 sl.st in the 1st ch, 1 sc in the 2nd ch, 1 hdc in the 3rd-6th ch, finish with a sl.st in the 20th sc of the round (so you skip 1 sc),

STEP 8. crochet 8 ch + 1 tch, turn around and crochet 1 sl.st in the 1st ch, 1 sc in the 2nd ch, 1 hdc in the 3rd ch, 1 dc in the 4th-8th ch, finish with a sl.st in the 23rd sc of the round (so you skip 2 sc),

STEP 9. crochet 4 ch + 1 tch, turn around and crochet 1 sl.st in the 1st ch, 1 sc in the 2nd ch, 1 hdc in the 3rd-4th ch, finish with a sl.st in the 25th sc of the round (so you skip 1 sc),

STEP 10. crochet 8 ch + 1 tch, turn around and crochet 1 sl.st in the 1st ch, 1 sc in the 2nd ch, 1 hdc in the 3rd ch, 1 dc in the 4th-8th ch, finish with a sl.st in the 28th sc of the round (so you skip 2 sc),

STEP 11. crochet 5 ch + 1 tch, turn around and crochet 1 sl.st in the 1st ch, 1 sc in the 2nd ch, 1 hdc in the 3rd-5th ch, finish with a sl.st in the 30th sc of the round (so you skip 1 sc)

Tie-off and leave enough yarn for sewing.

EARS

SPIKES (2X)

(Use yellow yarn)

RND 1: 6 sc in magic ring (6)

RND 2-3: 6 sc (6)

Tie-off with a sl.st.

OUTER EARS (2X)

(Use yellow yarn)

RND 1: 6 sc in magic ring (6)

RND 2: 6 sc (6)

RND 3: 2 sc in each 2nd sc (9)

RND 4-5: 9 sc (9)

RND 6: 2 sc in each 3rd sc (12)

RND 7-8: 12 sc (12)

RND 9: crochet around the spike and the ear (18)

RND 10-16: 18 sc (18)

RND 17: dec over each 5th and 6th sc (15)

COLLAR

OUTER EARS

INNER EARS

RND 18-19: 15 sc (15)

RND 20: dec over each 4th and 5th sc (12)

RND 21: 12 sc (12)

Tie-off with a sl.st and leave enough yarn for sewing.

INNER EARS (2x)

(Use black yarn)

ROW 1: 13 ch + 1 tch (13)

ROW 2: turn around and crochet 1 sl.st, 2 sc, 7 hdc, 2 sc, 1 sl.st. Continue on the other side of the chain, crochet 1 sl.st, 2 sc, 7 hdc, 2 sc, 1 sl.st

Tie-off and leave enough yarn for sewing.

SPIKES

HEAD

(Use yellow yarn)

STEP 1. crochet 3 ch + 1 tch, turn around and crochet 1 sl.st in the 1st ch, 1 sc in the 2nd-3rd ch,

STEP 2. crochet 5 ch + 1 tch, turn around and crochet 1 sl.st in the 1st ch, 1 sc in the 2nd ch, 1 hdc in the 3rd-4th ch, don't crochet in the 5th ch,

STEP 3. crochet 6 ch + 1 tch, turn around and crochet 1 sl.st in the 1st ch, 1 sc in the 2nd ch, 1 hdc in the 3rd-5th ch, don't crochet in the 6th ch,

STEP 4. crochet 5 ch + 1 tch, turn around and crochet 1 sl.st in the 1st ch, 1 sc in the 2nd ch, 1 hdc in the 3rd-4th ch, don't crochet in the 5th ch,

STEP 5. crochet 4 ch + 1 tch, turn around and crochet 1 sl.st in the 1st ch, 1 sc in the 2nd-3rd ch, don't crochet in the 4th ch

Tie-off and leave enough yarn for sewing.

ASSEMBLY

Sew the head to the body, at round 6 to round 12.

Sew the legs to the body. Sew the forelegs at round 7 to round 11, and the hind legs at round 21 to round 26.

To create the toes make two stitch lines with yellow yarn on the front of the feet, then pull them tight.

Cut four circles out of pink felt. Glue them to the bottom of the legs.

Sew the inner ears to the inside of the outer ears. Then sew the ears to the head, at round 7 to round 10.

Sew the spikes for the head to the top of the head, 1 round in front of the magic ring.

Put the white collar around the neck and sew the ends together.

Then put the yellow collar around the neck, and sew the ends together.

Sew the spikes for the head to the top of the head, 1 round in front of the magic ring.

Sew the spikes for the cheeks to both sides of the head, at round 11 to round 24.

FACE

Cut two eyes out of black and white felt. Glue them onto the head, at round 12 to round 15, with five stitches between the eyes.

Cut a nose out of black felt and glue it onto the head, at round 15.

Embroider a mouth to the head with thin black yarn, between rounds 17 and 18.

SPIKES HEAD

MEET THE AUTHOR

My name is Sabrina Somers. I live in the lovely city of Amsterdam in the Netherlands, with my husband Mark, our son Sven, our daughter Milou and two cats named Timmie and Sheila.

My crochet journey started back in 2014 when my husband bought me an amigurumi book as a gift. (Amigurumi is the incredibly popular Japanese art of crocheting small stuffed toys.) Thanks to that book I learned the different crochet stitches and I was able to create my first plush. By the end of 2014 I had made lots of different characters from various crochet books, and I was so taken with the craft that I decided to create my own amigurumi. By now I have designed over a 150 patterns and I love it!

I have been a big Pokémon fan since I was nine years old, I have literally lived with these incredible characters for years.

Who can forget the first time they saw Pikachu? I know I can't! It was love at first sight. I remember watching the TV series and following the adventures of Ash and Pikachu, and playing the games, first on the Game Boy and then on the DS. I loved the characters but most of all I loved the Pokémon themselves with all their wonderful colors and weird shapes.